PINNACLES AT BRYCE CANYON, BRYCE CANYON NATIONAL PARK

A symbol of Utah's incomparable

natural beauty, Delicate Arch catches

the desert sun's rich warm glow.

On any given evening throughout

the year, dozens of people from

around the world make the mile-

and-a-half pilgrimage to the arch,

which defies gravity on the rim of

its sandstone bowl. Visitation to

the arch has grown so dramatically

in recent years that the Park Service

has commissioned studies to assess

the impact of crowds on the park.

**DELICATE ARCH AT SUNSET,
ARCHES NATIONAL PARK**

UTAH

A CENTENNIAL CELEBRATION

PHOTOGRAPHY BY
TOM TILL

Tom Till

TEXT BY
BROOKE WILLIAMS

FOREWORD BY
TERRY TEMPEST WILLIAMS

PUBLISHED BY
WESTCLIFFE PUBLISHERS, INC.
ENGLEWOOD, COLORADO

THE COLORADO RIVER BENEATH FISHER TOWERS AND THE LA SAL MOUNTAINS, NEAR MOAB

EDITOR: Suzanne Venino

DESIGNER: Rebecca Finkel, F + P Graphic Design

PRODUCTION MANAGER: Suzanne Venino

ASSISTANT PRODUCTION MANAGER: Michelle R. Reeh

PHOTOGRAPHS © 1995 Tom Till.
ALL RIGHTS RESERVED.

TEXT © 1995 Brooke Williams.
ALL RIGHTS RESERVED.

FOREWORD © 1995 Terry Tempest Williams.
ALL RIGHTS RESERVED.

INTERNATIONAL STANDARD BOOK NUMBER:
1-56579-116-9

LIBRARY OF CONGRESS CATALOGUE NUMBER:
94-62089

PUBLISHED BY:
Westcliffe Publishers, Inc.
2650 South Zuni Street
Englewood, Colorado 80110

PRINTED IN SINGAPORE BY :
Tien Wah Press

NO PORTION OF THIS BOOK, EITHER
PHOTOGRAPHS OR TEXT, MAY BE REPRODUCED
IN ANY FORM WITHOUT THE WRITTEN
PERMISSION OF THE PUBLISHER.

ACKNOWLEDGMENTS

The photographs in this book are dedicated to my parents, George and Effie Till, who first brought me to Utah. Endless thanks to my family—Marcy, Mikenna, and Bryce—for their support, love, and patience. A number of the images in this volume would not have been possible without the scouting and logistical help of Glen Lathrop. Also, thanks to Dianne Howie, who helped push this project down the long pipeline, and to John Fielder and Suzanne Venino for their assistance. We greatly appreciate the business of our many stock clients worldwide who gave us the freedom to pursue this centennial book. And thanks to John Botkin of Photo Craft for processing my images. Statewide, thanks to the National Park Service, Bureau of Land Management, U.S. Forest Service, Utah State Parks and Recreation, Utah Statehood Centennial Commission, Theresa Cryns, Dana Carroll, Fred Cly, Bill and Monica Solawetz, Brooke and Terry Tempest Williams, and Ken Sanders. In Moab, thanks to Ann Carter, Steve Mulligan and Vicki Giglioti, Norm Shrewsbury at Westlight Photography, Karla VanderZander, and Canyonlands Field Institute.

— T. T.

FRONT COVER: WINTER LIGHT ON FIERY FURNACE WITH THE
LA SAL MOUNTAINS IN THE DISTANCE, ARCHES NATIONAL PARK

ALONG COYOTE GULCH, GLEN CANYON NATIONAL RECREATION AREA

A rare heavy snowfall blankets the Mittens and formations known as the Ansel Adams Rocks (foreground) in Monument Valley. This fantastic display of rock architecture introduced much of the world to the other-worldly beauty of the Colorado Plateau, as seen in the movie westerns of director John Ford and others. Monument Valley Tribal Park and San Juan County are part of the vast Navajo Reservation and home to a large Native American population. Living for centuries among some of the world's most spectacular scenery has found its expression in the chants and ceremonies of the Dineh, as the Navajos call themselves: "With beauty before him, With beauty behind him, With beauty above him, With beauty below him, All around him is beautiful, His spirit is all beautiful."

WINTER SUNRISE, MONUMENT VALLEY

MAKING VOWS
TERRY TEMPEST WILLIAMS

Wendell Berry writes, "If you know where you are, you know who you are." I believe Brooke Williams and Tom Till know both this country and themselves. They love Utah and they know it well. They especially know it well in their bodies. It is a part of them. I have hiked with these men. We are friends.

Brooke Williams is strong. He walks fast. As his wife, it is all I can do to keep up. Each step on the slickrock is a joy to him, each canyon a seduction toward further exploration. All seasons are game. Maps are memorized. Food is fuel. Instinct is his only true mentor.

Tom Till is a traveler of another sort. He walks into the country with his cameras on his back. His shadow on the sand appears as a modern day Kokopelli. It is not corn that he carries, but the seeds of his own perceptions. Tom is led by his eyes. He is a follower of light. He finds his way carefully into the heart of wilderness, stands in silence and waits for the land to reveal itself.

These men are obsessed, passionate, and foolish. They have quit traditional jobs—one a salesman, the other a teacher—in favor of new work rooted in the service and preservation of the wild lands they love. And so we have within these pages, the gifts, the stories, of a writer and a photographer who are offering us another way of being in the world, another way of seeing our centennial state.

Each chapter takes us further back in time, deep time, 100 years, 1,000 years, 10,000 years and beyond to the banks of Westwater Canyon where we can hold the black rocks of Precambrian granite in our hands. I feel the weight of questions: Could it be that we can project into the future only as far as we are willing to reflect back? How much of our past are we willing to consider? And is it possible to damage our days ahead by only knowing a part of the story or, as Williams writes, "to only see as far back as the people whose names we know."

Time. Space. Distance. Brooke Williams and Tom Till place us in correspondence with these ideas and offer us a visual perspective. As a people reflecting on Utah in this centennial year, I can think of nothing more valuable.

For most of our human history, people have been faced with one task, survival, and with one choice, life or death. Our species has done well. And now, technology has seen to it that we give birth more than we die. Our population is growing. By the year 2020, it is projected that in Utah there will be over three million of us.

We are now faced with many choices. How do we wish to live?

On February 19, 1947, Dr. Walter P. Cottam, a professor of botany at the University of Utah, delivered the eleventh annual Frederick William Reynolds Lecture entitled, "Is Utah Sahara Bound?" This address was given one hundred years after Brigham Young and the Mormon pioneers had entered the Salt Lake Valley. His message still stands:

> *This should be a festive year. It should also be year of serious reflection and meditation. Every citizen of this state who loves to call Utah home and who regards it as a permanent abode for his children and their posterity should become informed of the nature of the resources that support us and of what a century of white-man exploitation has done to them. Are we planning for the day when our obviously expendable resources…will have spent themselves? Are the potentially renewable resources of agriculture being managed on a sustained yield basis, or are they too being mined of their perpetual productivity? Can this civilization of ours, situated as it is in a semi-arid land, look with complacence to a permanently productive future when history speaks so repeatedly and so eloquently of failures of Old World civilizations nurtured in a similar desert environment? Must history repeat itself?*

We are living in a time of remarkable changes. The technology that has allowed us to be so successful, so comfortable and productive in our niche as a species is the same technology that is isolating us from what it means to be human. In the name of efficiency, we are losing our souls. Our computers, E-mail, Internet, fax machines, answering machines, cellular phones, and what appears daily on our television screens promise to bring us in greater relationship with the world around us. The designers of "the information highway" tell us this is our path toward the future.

BLAZING SUNSET REFLECTED IN A MOUNTAIN TARN, HIGH UINTAS WILDERNESS

RARE EXPANSE OF GLOBEMALLOW AFTER SPRING RAINS, SPANISH VALLEY

I do not believe them.

I believe our path toward the future is as it has always been—a people in a place with a commitment to community. Staying put. Slowing down. Listening. Learning the names of things: long-billed curlew, pronghorn antelope, black-tailed jackrabbit, short-horned lizard, sego lily, pinyon, juniper, sage. We must learn the names of our neighbors.

I believe we are a people in transition. We are moving from a largely rural frame of reference to an urban one. We must be careful and be mindful of our roots. If we do not stop and reflect upon what we are losing both physically and spiritually in terms of our relationship with the natural world and begin to extend our notion of community to include all life forms— plants, animals, rocks, rivers, soils, and human beings—then I fear we will be faced with a future of interminable loneliness, an unspeakable hunger for Other.

In this centennial year, may we take Dr. Cottam's words seriously and make both a personal and collective commitment to this place, Utah, that as a people we will listen to the land and to each other, that we will honor diversity and not fear our differences but use them for our greater understanding and compassion. May we make vows to sustain Utah's open spaces that we have been blessed with and not exploit them but use them respectfully as the gifts that they are. May we build beautiful towns and cities with strong cultural identities that have the capacity to integrate surrounding wilderness areas into our idea of civic responsibility, beauty, and health. May we not confuse progress with growth and recognize the courage of restraint. May we learn the stories of where we live and tell them to our children.

The black rocks of Westwater Canyon, the Precambrian granite we can hold in the palms of our hands, remind us how young we are and what brief residents in this country we have been.

Bless us in these years to come.

INSIDE THE ZION NARROWS, VIRGIN RIVER, ZION NATIONAL PARK

HIKER AND FALLS IN THE ZION NARROWS, ZION NATIONAL PARK

Winter fog inversions are a part of life in Utah, and it is a rare winter that does not include at least a number of days with low, steely gray skies and leaden air. In Moab, where people are accustomed to seeing the sun on a regular basis, the advent of a spell of the valley-choking winter mists can be a depressing experience. A drive up the La Sal Mountain Loop road can give immediate relief, as the vapors part at a certain elevation to reveal the world as it was before. The La Sal Mountains rise from the clouds like the buttressed coast of Big Sur, while their laccolithic brothers, the Henry Mountains, float above the sea of fog a hundred miles distant.

**FOG BELOW HIGH MESAS,
MANTI-LA SAL NATIONAL FOREST**

**PREVIOUS PAGE:
WARNER LAKE REFLECTS LA SAL MOUNTAINS,
MANTI-LA SAL NATIONAL FOREST**

MOVIE-SET GHOST TOWN NEAR THE PARIAH RIVER

It is July 24 and there are dozens of parades throughout Utah—parades in Provo and Ogden, South Jordan, Sandy, and in Salt Lake City the third largest parade in America is held. This is the parade that thousands of people came last night to wait for, with their sleeping bags and barbecues, lawn chairs and portable stereos. Today, floats and officials and marching bands and line after line of tapping tots file by beneath a sun that is hot enough to drill holes in any uncovered heads. Everyone is celebrating the day our ancestors first entered Salt Lake Valley. It is the same every year.

January 4 is another big day in Utah history, but there are no parades. It was the day one hundred years ago when word was received that, after six unsuccessful tries since 1849, Utah had become the forty-fifth state.

A half century after arriving in Utah, Mormons were still not considered American citizens because they practiced polygamy. Finally Mormon President Wilford Woodruff, acting for "the temporal salvation of the church," advised Latter-day Saints to "refrain from conducting any marriage forbidden by the Law of the land," thus clearing the way to statehood.

When the news of statehood came over the telegraph wire in 1896, the telegraph agent ran into the street, shooting his old shotgun into the air. As word spread, flags and decorations were hung in every store and home. An American flag was sewn, the new star lit from behind. The flag was big enough to cover the ceiling of the tabernacle, where the official announcement would be made and a gala ball held. Nearly everyone in town came, dressed more elegantly than ever, and danced.

Early January may not be the best time for parades and celebrations. But perhaps the real reason is that if you ask a hundred people the significance of January 4, only one or two might know the answer. To Mormons, and we are still mostly Mormons, statehood was a smaller beginning than that other day— July 24, 1847—almost fifty years earlier when Brigham Young, sick from a tick bite and months of dusty travel, strained to sit up in the back of Wilford Woodruff's wagon and said, "This is the right place."

While many restaurants are open on July 24 for holiday business and trash will still be collected, most offices and banks and industries are closed and no mail will be delivered. I leave our house three miles up Emigration Canyon at nine in the morning to hike in the foothills above Pioneer Trails State Park. I pass a dozen of the most sore-footed runners I've ever seen, four hours into the Deseret News Marathon, which follows a course similar to the one the first

A summer sunset paints an impressionistic canvas along the old Spanish Trail near Moab. The earliest settlers of the aptly named Spanish Valley reported they found a well-used trail beneath the La Sal Mountains when they arrived. On a map, this route between New Mexico and California is hardly a straight line, bowing up hundreds of miles to avoid the maze of Colorado River canyons and mesas that begin in the Behind-the-Rocks escarpment, which rises 3,000 feet above the valley floor.

SUNSET ABOVE THE LA SAL MOUNTAINS

WAGON AND RAMADA, WITH MONUMENT VALLEY IN DISTANCE, GOULDINGS TRADING POST

Mormons traversed on the last days of their trek. From the looks of these last runners, they are trying to duplicate on one hot summer morning, the pain and suffering of that entire first four-month journey.

I park at the mouth of the canyon and begin walking up a dusty trail. The oak is green, but the few other plants living here are yellow and dry and scratch my legs. In an hour I am sitting on a sandstone ledge, marking the top of an unnamed summit, with the valley spread out below me like a picnic. I can see clearly the gridded roads, straight and perfect enough to set your compass. To the south there is a canyon and a green mountain and another canyon and mountain and another and another as the ridge turns to the west, forming the lip of this giant bowl.

This Is The Place State Park is directly below me. Pioneer houses have been moved in and fields planted and tilled using horses. Familiar Lombardi poplars, columnar like green missiles, mark some of the plots. Emigration Creek is lush with healthy cottonwoods. Below bright yellow slopes splattered with dark green stands of oak, condominiums have sprouted on Donner Hill.

I try to imagine how the valley looked one hundred and fifty years ago, all flat and yellow in the summer—and dry. There was one cedar tree. Vandals cut it down but a monument to it has been erected on Third South and Sixth East Streets. I imagine the streams running out of every canyon, like flat veins spreading life around the valley. The streams are all out of sight, in pipes now.

To the north, a huge hospital complex marks the east edge of the valley, spreading into Fort Douglas and Research Park, with all its flat, modern buildings. Below me and beyond I can see the horizon and the Great Salt Lake, almost a mirage, and Salt Lake City filling all the valley between there and here and spilling out the sides. What would Brigham think of what has become of this "right place?" Did he have any idea what he was starting? There is one clue that I think suggests he did.

Before his death, Brigham left a note with his burial instructions, which Leonard Arrington included in his book, *Brigham Young, American Moses:*

> *I want my coffin made of plump 1¼ inch redwood boards, not scrimped in length, but two inches longer than I would measure, and from two to three inches wider than is commonly made for a person of my breadth and size…to have the appearance that if I wanted to turn a little to the right or left I should have plenty of room to do so…*

Brigham thought of everything, it seems, even having his coffin made big enough to allow him to turn over in his grave.

By the time the Mormons arrived in Salt Lake Valley, the way was well worn. Fur trappers, looking for beaver to fill the growing demand for pelt hats, discovered trails that would eventually be used by early settlers, including the Mormons. The Pony Express followed the same routes, which would one day become major highways.

The Cache and Salt Lake Valleys were explored in the 1820s. Jim Bridger discovered the Great Salt Lake in 1824 or 1825, believing it to be an arm of the Pacific Ocean. In 1841, the Bartleson-Bidwell group brought the first wagons through Utah. They came thinking that a river ran out the south end of Great Salt Lake that they could float all the way to San Francisco. John C. Fremont made his first of five journeys to Utah in 1842. His explorations helped to dispel rumors and contributed information that would later be invaluable to the peopling of the West. Journals from his 1845 expedition describing the fertile valleys west of the Wasatch Mountains became a major factor in Brigham Young's decision to bring the Mormons to the Salt Lake Valley.

The Donner Party, following poor information, chose what they thought was a shortcut along the Hastings Cutoff, instead of taking the traditional route along the Oregon Trail. The time spent blazing this route southwest of Fort Bridger and across the hot and muddy Great Salt Lake Desert contributed to disaster at Donner Summit the following winter. Eleven months after the Donner Party entered the Salt Lake Valley, the Mormons followed the same route.

On April 5, 1847, when 149 handpicked Mormon "souls" left Nebraska for Utah with 73 wagons, 93 horses, 52 mules, 66 oxen, 19 cows, 17 dogs, a cannon, a boat, and some chickens, they were accustomed to moving. Because of the continued persecution they had endured throughout their young history, the Mormons had moved from New York, where the Church of Jesus Christ of Latter-day Saints was founded in 1830, to Ohio, to Illinois, to Winter Quarters, Nebraska. Two thousand Mormons lived in Kirkland, Ohio, by 1835. A decade later, 12,000 lived in Nauvoo, Illinois, including 5,000 new converts from Great Britain. They remained loyal to the United States Constitution but they lived according to a government under God, and God's spokesman was their prophet, Joseph Smith. This threatened the local, non-Mormon population.

On August 7, 1842, Joseph Smith was drinking a glass of cold water when, according to witnesses, the color of his face changed to a brilliant white and he gazed off into the distance and said that the water he was drinking tasted much like that of the crystal streams running from the snow-capped mountains. He said, "I am gazing upon the valleys of those mountains," and he followed with a vivid description. Joseph Smith prophesied that "the saints would continue to suffer much affliction and would be driven to the Rocky Mountains, many would apostatize, others would be put to death by our persecutors, or lose their lives in consequence of exposure or disease; and some of you will live to go and assist in making settlements and build cities and see the saints become a mighty people in the midst of the Rocky Mountains."

Two years later, Joseph Smith and his brother Hyrum were jailed for inciting a riot among dissenters who denounced plural marriage and other Mormon practices. They were killed when local militia broke into their jail cells and shot them. Brigham Young became the new Mormon prophet. Believing that they were on the verge of disaster, he made plans to move his people west to a place where they could live in peace.

Prior to the Mormons, most travelers had come to the Salt Lake Valley by mistake: Jim Bridger thinking he had arrived at the Pacific Ocean; the Bartleson-Bidwells to float a non-existent

ABANDONED CABIN, OPHIR

In the desert mountain ranges of central

Utah, the aspen tree has evolved into

one of the world's most remarkable living

things. Besides being home to some of the

tallest and biggest aspen trees in the world,

the Great Basin mesas also support what

some scientists believe may be the world's

largest living entity: giant groves of trees

that share a common root system. The

biomass of these groves far surpasses that

of any individual sequoia tree or even

animals such as elephants or blue whales.

The inner workings of these giant organisms

are fascinating, with nutrients and water

shifted underground from healthy trees to

other individuals who are less well off.

**ASPEN GROVE AND SPLIT-RAIL FENCE,
MANTI-LA SAL NATIONAL FOREST**

river; the Donners on a shortcut that cost many of them their lives. According to the journals of a few of those first Mormon settlers, their journey to the Salt Lake Valley was also a mistake.

Lorenzo Young arrived ill, exhausted, and in a bad mood after 110 days on the trail. "I felt heartsick," he wrote. Harriet, his wife, wrote, "we have travelled fifteen hundred miles to get here, and I would willingly travel a thousand miles farther to get where it looked as though a white man could live." In contrast, Thomas Bullock wrote in his journal about the clear sky and delightful air and "oceans of stone" to use for building houses. He also noted the absence of timber. Orson Pratt and Erastus Snow, sent ahead of the main group with instructions to search "out a suitable place for putting in our seed," arrived in the valley on July 21. Pratt wrote a detailed description of the valley in his journal:

> After going into the valley about five miles, we turned our course to the north, down toward the Salt Lake. For 3 or 4 miles north we found the soil of a most excellent quality. Streams from the mountains and springs were very abundant, the water excellent, and generally with gravel bottoms. A great variety of green grass, and very luxuriant, covered the bottoms for miles where the soil was sufficiently damp, but in other places, although the soil was good, yet the grass had nearly dried up for want of moisture. We found the drier places swarming with very large crickets, about the size of a man's thumb. As we proceeded toward the salt lake the soil began to assume a more sterile appearance, being at some seasons of the year overflowed with water. We found as we proceeded on, great numbers of hot springs issuing from near the base of the mountains….We travelled for about 15 miles down after coming into the valley, the latter parts of the distance, the soil being unfit for agricultural purposes.

When the first Mormons entered the Salt Lake Valley they entered a wilderness. Within two days City Creek had been dammed and diverted to irrigate large plots of land where beans, buckwheat, turnips, corn, and potatoes were planted. By the time Brigham Young's detachment arrived, a small community was already buzzing with activity. Within a week a road was built to haul wood cut from a nearby canyon, a blacksmith shop was set up, and hunters and fishermen were sent out for food. By the seventh day Brigham Young had decided on a site for the temple and had laid out plans for a city in 135 ten-acre blocks. A three-acre plot had turned bright green with sprouting corn. By the third week, 29 houses had been built. A steady stream of settlers began arriving and by September 1848, more than 3,000 people lived in the valley.

In 1849, Brigham Young's first plural wife, Lucy Decker, arrived in Salt Lake with her young son, Brigham. She would give birth to six more children. The last, Clarissa, (we call her Clicky) was my great grandmother. According to *Brigham Young at Home*, the book Clarissa Young Spencer wrote about her father:

> [In 1851] the Saints met in conference and voted to begin building the Temple. They were still destitute and struggling day in and day out to make a home in the wilderness, but they made plans to erect an edifice which was eventually to cost four million dollars and take forty years to complete. Do I praise too highly when I call such courage and vision magnificent?

SPRING ORCHARD BLOOMS, CAPITOL REEF NATIONAL PARK

MCPHERSON RANCH REMAINS, DESOLATION CANYON

By 1857, one hundred towns had been established in Utah and by 1868, another hundred, including some in southern Idaho and southeast Arizona. In 1877, when Brigham Young died, the hard work had been done.

In my mind I can see a photograph of him taken about 1873. He is sitting in a chair, his right arm resting on a wooden table with his top hat sitting on it, his left arm holding a cane as if a moment before he was ready to get up but decided he was too comfortable. He seems settled in, slightly slumped, and his eyes seem to be dreaming. It is a picture of a man who has mostly done what he set out to do.

In the state capitol rotunda, there is a bust of Brigham Young. He looks older than the photograph and has eyes that seemed mean and scary to me as a young boy. The plaque sums up his life: Brought 100,000 people to Utah. Established 300 communities. Built canals, railroads, Temples. Founded banks, stores, industries, institutions. Governor 1850–1858. Beloved by his people.

He left a nation when he died.

In 1994, a new statue of Brigham Young was installed in the rotunda and now when I think of him, this statue is what I see. He is younger, forty-something, in a confident walk. The statue is facing south. (I think they should turn it west.) He is in the middle of a long stride and is carrying a stout stick in his left hand. His legs are like trees and he has high boots. The look in his eye is off to the left as if he is thinking. His hair is swept back—the wind might be blowing—and a strong right hand is thrown forward with its fingers bent and relaxed. This statue is full of hope and embodies everything he would do or dream of in his life. This statue is nine feet tall. Life sized.

GHOST TOWN OF GRAFTON, WITH ZION CLIFFS IN BACKGROUND

SPRING VERDURE AND FALLS, ZION NATIONAL PARK

CORRALS AND BUTTES IN THE SAN RAFAEL SWELL

OPPOSITE: FACTORY BUTTE AND SURROUNDING BADLANDS IN WINTER, PROPOSED SAN RAFAEL WILDERNESS

Utah's ghost towns are some of the state's most valuable historical resources and also some of the most endangered. Easy prey for vandalism, both natural and human, many of the best have deteriorated greatly in recent years. One of the buildings in Grafton was burned several years ago, and heavy snows in 1993 collapsed roofs on buildings along the spine of the Wasatch Range. Thistle is perhaps Utah's newest ghost town, destroyed when a huge mud- and landslide in Spanish Fork Canyon formed a natural dam that flooded the old railroad town.

OLD RAILROAD STATION IN THISTLE

COVERED WAGONS BELOW THE WASATCH MOUNTAINS, THIS IS THE PLACE STATE PARK, SALT LAKE CITY

OPPOSITE: TWILIGHT ON TEMPLE SQUARE, SALT LAKE CITY

A summer rainbow arcs above Salt Lake

City, 147 years after the Mormon Saints

entered through the Wasatch Mountains,

which rise above the city in the distance.

An oasis surrounded by a fearsome desert,

Salt Lake City and the Wasatch Front make

a long, thin 200-mile strip of civilization

at the base of the towering fault block

range. Most precipitation in the area falls

during summer thunderstorms, like the

one shown here, and during winter snow

storms, which can be fueled by the warm

waters of the nearby Great Salt Lake.

RAINBOW OVER SALT LAKE CITY

ANASAZI RUIN, CANYONLANDS NATIONAL PARK

At first, Glen doesn't believe me about the kiva.

We have followed a canyon rim and a dry, deep wash looking for anything and nothing, just walking. On the surface, this hike seems typical of many Glen and I have made to this blank and useless part of modern Utah. But down farther, in the undercurrent of my life, this trip is different. It has been a month since my young mother died from a clot in the back of her heart, and for a month I have hidden from people in grocery stores not wanting to talk and I had smiled painful smiles to comfort those who had never faced death. Glen knew I needed a long, sweaty walk.

I had barely listened when Glen talked on the phone about this canyon, one of the few left he hadn't explored. In the canyons of the Colorado Plateau, there are still discoveries to be made. People like Glen spend their free time hiking and collecting magic places and stubbornly pass information among themselves. He'd been studying his topographic maps and traded some of his secrets for hints from friends who knew about this place, and he seemed to have the way memorized. No one had ever mentioned the kiva.

We met in Moab yesterday afternoon and drove a few hours south and then west into the sun, which shot through my bug-covered windshield like a laser. Instead of stopping to clean it, I drove the last miles with my head out the window, to see the rocks and ruts better, but more to let the wind blow into my brain and clear away the pieces of death that would not fit into my heart—all the noise and speculation and selfish belief that I knew were only escapes, cheap ways to mask a pain I needed to learn how to feel.

The light died about the same time as the road broke up and slowed us to a speed that wouldn't measure on my speedometer. So we stopped, threw out our bags, and went to sleep. I didn't dream once.

We are somewhere in the middle of the Dark Canyon Wilderness Study Area, 126,000 acres of the 5.7-million-acre Utah BLM Wilderness Bill. The map shows two forks to this canyon, with the road down the center. By ten this morning we had walked to the end of the road and found our way down to a flat, whitish layer that formed the top of a solid, vertical wall. By noon we had wandered a mile along the wall looking for a crack that might lead to the bottom. Occasionally, I found myself standing as far out on the edge as was safe, staring down at an abyss like a horrible mysterious wound.

It was spitting hot by the time the wall broke up and we made our own way down through giant talus, ledge to ledge to the bottom. Water was long gone and the mud had faint green shadows from old moss. Dead pools were black with bodies of tadpoles who were too slow turning to frogs. We had left our packs at the confluence in a tiny spot of shade and had wandered a half mile looking for water when Glen looked up and noticed a small wall of stacked stones high in a southwest facing alcove.

PICTOGRAPH, NATURAL BRIDGES NATIONAL MONUMENT

ANCIENT PICTOGRAPHS, SOUTHERN UTAH

PREVIOUS PAGE: AUGUST SUNSET ABOVE MONUMENT BASIN AND THE NEEDLES, CANYONLANDS NATIONAL PARK

We climbed loose red dirt and the faces of huge boulders tilted to the edge of traction and used solid branches for balance to get beyond what we thought was an insurmountable vertical wall. Then we climbed one hundred feet of talus like a ladder, forgetting the dead, hot air in the bottom, which had given way to a barely perceptible twisting breeze. I got there first, breathing hard, to find a small village hidden where the high, curving wall of the alcove met the flat floor.

"Glen," I say, trying to whisper and still make him hear, "the most perfect kiva." I'm referring to other "perfect" kivas we've found by following maps drawn on napkins and our own imaginations. He thinks I'm kidding until he sees it.

The outside wall is chest high, four feet, built of similar sized rocks, larger than bricks, fit together with mud mortar. The kiva is not perfectly round because its back is the surface of the alcove wall. The top is perfectly flat and the only indication that it has been here a long time is that the mud covering the branches laid between the cross poles has shrunk slightly and pulled away from the canyon wall. The opening in the roof is a perfect square formed by three large sandstone tiles. There is no ladder. Curiously, three small stairs have been built on the outside wall, maybe for a crippled elder needed in the kiva. There is a hole in the top of the wall, a ventilation shaft down to the fire pit.

I don't feel like going in at first, but wander along the shelf. There are six other rooms, some totally intact. There are black and white potsherds everywhere, some bigger than the palm of my hand. There are hundreds of small corncobs. There are no footprints.

This small village might have been built during the Development Pueblo Period, sometime between 1,300 and 900 years ago. This period is known for textiles and domesticated turkeys and single-story structures built on the surface. The kivas of this time evolved from the pit houses built by Modified Basket Makers during the previous period, when the people began using bows and arrows and planting kidney beans and varied strains of corn. The Basket Maker Period began around A.D. 300 and marked the beginning of agriculture in the area, which meant that the people became more stationary, allowing them the luxury of permanent dwellings and time for making beautiful baskets.

I try to imagine the thousands of similar small villages in this area, which is now part of a county less populated than during Anasazi times. Around A.D. 1050, the Great Period began with burgeoning Anasazi populations migrating and congregating in the huge multi-storied, many-roomed buildings of places like Chaco, Betatakin, and Mesa Verde. The Great Period marked the zenith for the Anasazi and lasted until A.D. 1300 when, because of enemy raids or extended droughts, the people— the "Guardians of the Lifeway"—moved south to Arizona where their great-great grandchildren now live as Zunis and Hopis, and men still descend into kivas where "cosmic regions intersect, where the heartbeat of the earth is felt."

When it is time to go down into the kiva, I step on the three steps carefully, sit down on the edge of the entrance, and dangle my legs in the darkness. The roof supports my weight without the slightest quiver. I feel places for my feet and climb down. I find my way to the back and as my eyes adjust I sit down. I feel strange and foreign. I imagine men sweating from the heat of the fire deflected by the flat stone that now lies broken. I can smell them. I can see the hole, the *sipapu*, in front of me, where the inner and outer mix, where conscious meets unconscious, the symbol of the place where first man and first woman came into the world. I almost hear children outside, and dogs and songs, and a woman grinding seeds between two stones. I tuck myself into the corner where the man-made wall meets the canyon. I can see where the mortar was pushed between rocks by fingers the same size as mine and these last thousand years seem like nothing.

It is time to be careful not to think that I can possibly know these people from their broken vessels and abandoned buildings. In my mind the mark in the old mud grows a finger, then a hand and arm, and in a minute I see an entire young male body and then elders and dancing and I feel the fire. Here where the worlds meet I am aware of a complete and rarified silence and I realize that this is what I've come for. This is what is missing from my life, the silence to let death be. The quiet vibrates like the noiseless wings of a hundred invisible insects. Here, for the first time since her death, I see in my mind my mother's bright thin face and not the puffy, pale, dead one that has turned my life into a nightmare. Here, where the worlds meet, that nightmare ends. I sit for a while, then, when I'm ready, I climb out and enter a world that has somehow renewed itself. It is so bright I can't look without squinting and color explodes inside my eyes.

Wilderness is many things. It is a place, according to the Wilderness Act of 1964, "where earth and community of life are untrammeled by man, where man himself is a visitor who does not remain." It is where to go to merge with the place we came from and learn to live, if only for a day or a week, how we have always lived. It is a place to go when our mothers die and nothing else will work.

FINS AND ROCK FORMATIONS, BEHIND-THE-ROCKS WILDERNESS STUDY AREA

SNAKE PETROGLYPH, SAN RAFAEL SWELL

OPPOSITE: IMPOSING SANDSTONE TEETH OF THE SAN RAFAEL SWELL, PROPOSED SAN RAFAEL SWELL WILDERNESS

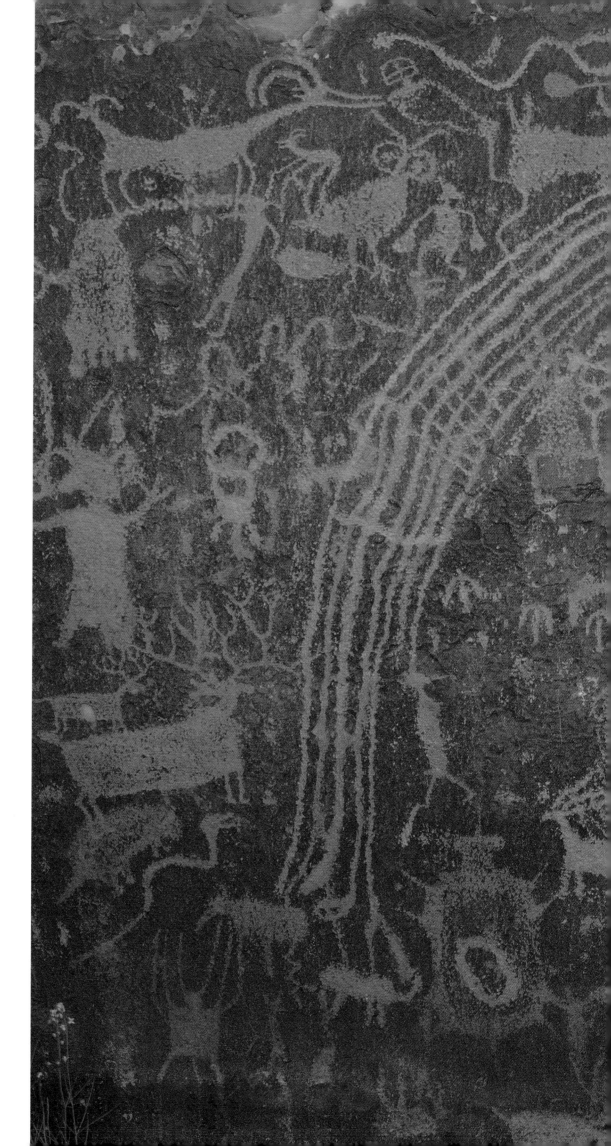

No state has more ancient Native American petroglyphs and pictographs than Utah. Thousands of rock art panels cover the sandstone in almost every county, embodying styles from thousands of years in the past to paintings on stone done by modern Ute artists. Sometimes the art consists of a few isolated figures, while at other times the frescos cover huge walls with complex shapes and symbols that may require hours for the visitors to take in. Unfortunately some of the best art—including the Moab Panel near Moab, petroglyphs along the San Juan River, and numerous panels in Buckhorn Wash in the San Rafael Swell—have been badly damaged by visitors. In 1994, rangers at Lake Powell also reported extensive vandalism to many of the panels that escaped drowning by Lake Powell, and they vowed to get tougher on the criminals who are destroying such an important part of Utah's historical heritage.

PETROGLYPH PANEL, CENTRAL UTAH

DAWN VIEW OF SAN RAFAEL SWELL, PROPOSED SAN RAFAEL SWELL WILDERNESS

KOKOPELLI AND SHEEP PETROGLYPHS, SOUTHERN UTAH

Tucked in an alcove of a distant canyon

in San Juan County, an ancient ruin still

stands, its timbers and mortar mellowed

by vast amounts of time. There are many

mysteries surrounding the ancient native

people who lived in these canyons: what

of their religion, their social structure,

their arts, their daily lives? And, most

mysterious of all, what caused them to

give up their homes and leave this vast

beautiful desert, never to return.

TWENTY-ROOM RUIN, SAN JUAN COUNTY

INDIAN PAINTBRUSH, ARCHES NATIONAL PARK

OPPOSITE: KACHINA BRIDGE SHELTERS A SMALL RUIN, NATURAL BRIDGES NATIONAL MONUMENT

IMPOSING WALLS OF HOVENWEEP CASTLE, HOVENWEEP NATIONAL MONUMENT

MITCHELL BUTTE AND THE SETTING MOON, MONUMENT VALLEY TRIBAL PARK, NAVAJO RESERVATION

A PAST AND PRESENT LAKE

It hasn't snowed for weeks. Here, on top of Mount Raymond (10,365 feet), I can hear the wind moan down in the trees just seconds before it shoots me with ice crystals that sting and freeze my face. The morning sun doesn't help.

A mile below me Salt Lake Valley is invisible, sleeping beneath a blue-gray blanket of fog. Every few years, a high pressure system creates a temperature inversion that traps moisture from condensing snow in the valley, where it mixes with chimney smoke and vehicle emissions. A fog forms, thick enough to block the sun and deep enough to seem like water.

A few days of this and people's brains go haywire, and I realize that we need light almost as much as we need air. When this weather comes, I try to leave the valley whenever I can, but a haywired brain makes it easy to stay home, forgetting that the entire world is not drowned in fog.

I like to ski. In fact, I love to ski and I am not alone. Here in Utah we have the "Greatest Snow on Earth" and if you don't believe it, just look at our license plates. But today, this snow is not the greatest on Earth or anywhere else. While the valley has been filled by smog, the sun has been baking these mountains and the snow has melted every day and refrozen at night, and skis don't make a mark until mid morning. Skiing perfect snow is not why I came today. I did not come here to take long runs in a rhythm that is dance married to flight through snow so light it must be what the floor of heaven is made of. Not today. An eye-blue sky and air the temperature of spring make it easy to forget perfect skiing.

This morning, just past dawn, clicking into my bindings, I crossed the line separating my two lives. I must spend most of my time on the side where everything gets taken care of, where I work and try to live smoothly, where the walks get shoveled and bills get paid. I share this life with millions.

The other side is my own—the sweating and the one foot in front of the other, the rhythm and the getting somewhere tall and broad where I find something that might not be there without me. Today the biggest cloud in the world has brought Lake Bonneville back, just for me.

Climbing to ten thousand feet has taken me back ten thousand years to a time when the most recent of the Pleistocene lakes was waning. It was colder then and wetter, and more than fifty Ice-Age glaciers, some that were twelve miles long, were carving these canyons. One, in Little Cottonwood Canyon, was calving icebergs, which would float off toward the middle of Lake Bonneville. Fourteen-thousand years ago, this lake reached a level so high that it overflowed just north of Red Rock Pass in Idaho. Between then and now, this region has been more dry than wet and Lake Bonneville, which may have covered 6,000 square miles at one time, evaporated several times. Now the remnant, the Great Salt Lake, fluctuates in size between 2,300 and 1,000 square miles.

I once saw the Great Salt Lake on a picture of Earth taken from space. It stood out clearly, and even without political boundaries drawn in, I knew where I lived.

SANDSTONE FINS IN WINTER,
BEHIND-THE-ROCKS WILDERNESS

OPPOSITE: WINTER THISTLES BENEATH
MOUNT TIMPANOGOS, UTAH VALLEY

An autumn storm leaves a wet coating of snow at the mouth of Little Cottonwood Canyon. Two of the scenic wonders of Utah, Big and Little Cottonwood Canyons in the Wasatch Mountains also provide watershed for the Salt Lake Valley and are the center for Utah's famed ski resorts. Polished white granite rises steeply above the deep cleft of Little Cottonwood, culminating in the high basins of Lone Peak Wilderness.

EARLY SNOW IN LITTLE COTTONWOOD CANYON

Geologists study the Great Salt Lake because locked up in its sediments may be the most complete climatic record on earth. They say that it is best to think of the Great Salt Lake as a "temporary stage that began millions of years in the past and will continue through the foreseeable future." A few wet centuries and a degree or two drop in yearly average temperatures and Lake Bonneville will be back full of water, not fog.

Now, temporarily, we have the Great Salt Lake and it is part of all of our lives. It reddens and liquifies our sunsets. When the wind blows, we can smell it from across the valley, the deep, earthy smells of things churning and changing and renewing themselves.

There are islands in the Great Salt Lake—some with nothing but nesting pelicans and rocks, some with beaches more wild than Mexico. Marshes line the shores of the lake and more than our share of the world's birds land there during their migrations. Humans have hunted and gathered there until almost recently. Beginning 10,000 years ago, when Paleo-Indians killed mammoths and Ice Age camels with fluted points, and ending as recently as fifty years ago, when Proto-Shoshones hunted antelope and mule deer, people have constantly used the birds and muskrats, bulrushes, pickleweed, and cattails of the lush marshes that have migrated as the waters of the Great Salt Lake rose and fell.

The Great Salt Lake is in charge of the weather here. Thirsty storms cross California and dry out over Nevada before sucking water from the warmer lake. Then, drunk and slow, these storms slam into the Wasatch Range on the east side of the valley, and lift themselves, up and over, and abandon their wet ballast over the mountains. We drink these storms. We ski them.

I begin to chill and notice the sun has moved higher. Then I remember to go to work. Lake Bonneville turns back into fog. I think I'll go down the southern ridge to some north-facing shade I can see in the distance. With luck, I might find loose, sugary snow where I can make some turns. In a minute, I'm down off the summit and I notice a lone coyote's tracks and wonder what in the world was a coyote doing up here? Slipping along the rim of a huge bowl, my ski edges scratch the snow, which isn't much softer than when I climbed up. Ten more minutes of that and I'm suddenly cold, in the shade. I actually sink a few inches into the loose snow—hoar, they call it. Hoar becomes depthhoar when new snow falls on top of it. Enough weight on the depthhoar from new snow, or maybe a skier, and the whole slope avalanches. It is difficult to know when. In Salt Lake City on winter mornings, many radio stations air more avalanche forecasts than traffic reports.

I know I'm smiling because I've found a clear, long line between trees, and I push off into my first of twenty wide, fast turns. My skis make noise as they cut through the icy crystals. I make good time with gravity helping me and in a half hour I've reached the car, loaded my gear, and started down the canyon. I reach the cloud in five miles. Back in my office, I've barely been missed.

I don't do well in the city. I feel better in wild places, in any season, at altitudes that make me think when I breathe, where I can see big pictures and have big dreams. Places where I might see an eagle. But if I must live in a valley, Salt Lake may be the best one. The ties that bind me here are loose. The good thing about coming down, maybe the only good thing, is wondering how long it will be before I go back up.

BIG SPRING GUSHES FROM A CANYON WALL
IN ZION NARROWS, ZION NATIONAL PARK

SILVER ISLAND MOUNTAINS REFLECTED IN STANDING POOLS, BONNEVILLE SALT FLATS

SALT PATTERNS, BONNEVILLE SALT FLATS

PLAYA LEFT BEHIND BY RECEDING LAKE WATERS, ANTELOPE ISLAND STATE PARK

SUNSET COLORED BY FOREST FIRE SMOKE, ANTELOPE ISLAND STATE PARK

ANTELOPE ISLAND SURROUNDED BY LAKE WATERS, ANTELOPE ISLAND STATE PARK

SPRING BLOOMS ABOVE RED BUTTE GARDENS, OUTSIDE OF SALT LAKE CITY

PENSTEMON IN PROFUSION, SKYLINE DRIVE, WASATCH MOUNTAINS

The white granites of the Wasatch

Mountains take on the crimson cast of

sunset in this aerial view. Most of the

peaks in the photograph lie in the Lone

Peak Wilderness, the first congressionally

designated wilderness in Utah. Hiking

from the Salt Lake Valley to the cirque

below Lone Peak's summit is equivalent

to hiking the Grand Canyon bottom to

top. But instead of the gentle switch-

backs of the trails in the Grand Canyon,

here the 5,600-foot elevation gain and loss

occurs in under four miles, one of the

steepest hiking trails in the West.

LONE PEAK WILDERNESS, WASATCH MOUNTAINS

MAPLES AND OAKS IN MORNING LIGHT, UINTA NATIONAL FOREST

OPPOSITE: RAINBOW IN THE MISTS OF BRIDALVEIL FALLS, PROVO CANYON

Big Cottonwood Creek rushes beneath a forest canopy near Lake Blanche Fork. The canyons of the Wasatch Mountains continue to be issues in the battle over resource protection and development. Pressures on the fragile riparian areas are especially great, as more than a million people now reside within miles of this location. There are few places on earth where so many live so close to so much wilderness, and the next one hundred years will offer choices that will either doom the canyons or provide for their preservation.

FALLS IN BIG COTTONWOOD CANYON,
WASATCH NATIONAL FOREST

It is late summer in southern Utah's canyon country, only this is not a canyon. It is one of the many mesa tops you see while driving south on lonely straight highways, and the kink in your neck makes you turn and look out the car window. If these mesas have names, I've never bothered to learn them. Looking west from a distance, this one is a great, jagged green line of trees marking the top of a Navajo sandstone dome that has been flattened by time and weather. Bob Helms and I are here to see what the American West looked like before people brought their livestock here to feed. We are bent down in the shade of a huge old juniper gathering ghost beads. We know fall is around the corner by the pile jackets we are wearing this morning, by looking south where aspens have yellowed just the tops of high hills, and by small birds flying in groups.

Yesterday we drove into Moab and spent ten minutes finding a parking place at a new restaurant. We drank some fancy, fruit-flavored beer while they cleaned the mountain bikers away from our table. We ate a very strange pizza (roasted garlic, goat cheese, and peppers, on a wheat crust) and then drove out of town. We passed four brand new motels (No Vacancy), bike, art, and book shops, a huge supermarket, and the new equestrian center. An hour and a half later we were at the end of a rocky dirt road. Before throwing out my sleeping bag, I spent five minutes clearing away cow pies, kicking down twenty hard lumps where grasses once grew, and filling ten hoof prints made during the last rain storm, which I'm sure this land can't remember.

I woke up after a nightmare about being an outfielder in a baseball game. The bases were loaded. All I can remember is my panic when I couldn't let go of the ball as I tried to throw it, and opposing players just kept scoring. This is a recurring dream. A therapist once told me it meant that my sub-conscious was telling me I needed to let go of something if I was to keep the opposition from scoring. Bob, I found out later was dreaming, too, about his friend Smokey's brother-in-law flipping Bob's raft in the Grand Canyon. "It was not a significant dream," Bob told me. "Smokey's brother-in-law always flips rafts."

I woke up this morning in a very foreign place. Bob was camped on a flat spot in the road with his gear spread out around him, heating water on his stove. Right around me was nothing but grasses chewed down to ground level, some straggly looking sage, and scratchy Russian thistle lining the road. A hundred feet away some anemic juniper trees were growing, but that was it. Looking east, as far as I could see, it was worse. The whole place seemed to have just barely survived something big and horrid. If there is a "War on the West," we spent the night on one of the battlefields.

Bob is the quintessential desert rat. He owns a small adventure company and a garage full of gear. He takes conservation groups, school kids, and individuals on river trips and backpacking in remote parts of the Colorado Plateau. He has spent the last twenty-five years in southern Utah and if you want to see his hackles stand up, mention ranching and mining as traditional uses of this land.

WINTER MOON RISE, CASTLE ROCK

OPPOSITE: STORMY LIGHT OVER THE COLORADO CANYONS, FROM DEAD HORSE POINT STATE PARK

Tukuhnikivatz Peak in the La Sal

Mountains is seen through a small

natural sandstone arch. The pyramidal

peak is the focal point of one chapter

of Edward Abbey's classic, DESERT

SOLITAIRE, and integral to the book's

closing scene. As Abbey leaves Moab,

a storm momentarily lifts: "For a few

minutes the whole region from the

Canyon of the Colorado to the Book

Cliffs—crag, mesa, turret, dome,

canyon wall, plain, swale and dune—

glows with a vivid amber light against

the darkness to the east. At the same

time I see a mountain peak rising clear

of the clouds, old Tukuhnikivatz fierce

as the Matterhorn, snowy as Everest,

invincible."

NATURAL ARCH FRAMES THE
LA SAL MOUNTAINS, BEHIND-THE ROCKS
WILDERNESS STUDY AREA

BEE FLOWERS AT PAROWAN GAP, GREAT BASIN

Bob knows that traditional uses go back way beyond the hundred-and-fifty years white people have been making their living cutting chunks out of the west.

To Bob, traditional uses are wandering, exploring (snooping, he calls it,) hunting, gathering, camping under trees, wading brown rivers, walking at night guided by stars, knowing whose tracks are whose, and stringing necklaces from beads made from the seeds of blue juniper berries. Bob has made necklaces for all of his friends and one of his necklaces is buried with his business partner's young daughter. Navajos call these beads "Juniper's eyes." They only take the ones with a hole in one end, those which have already been broken into by small animals. Some say Navajos never go anywhere without a string of these beads, which they believe help them find their way at night. They also believe that the beads prevent nightmares by reminding those who carry them of the bond between tree and animal and man.

Bob makes his living teaching "traditional uses" and he understands that knowing what time has done to this country is good for our modern lives and that we are better after spending time between rocks and under stars. Bob knows we need it. In a sense, Bob has bet his life on this place.

We ate oatmeal and put our gear in the car, locked it, and walked off toward a corner of the mesa where the rock had eroded into cracks and blocks. We were on the mesa top in twenty minutes.

We were in a different country, a new wild country. Crossing the wild border is usually emotional, personal, where something risky or dangerous begins, where life gets extreme. It might be just a feeling. But today, this wild border is one hundred feet of steep white rock. Pretty obvious.

At first, we walked the rocky edge, not wanting to touch anything. Pinyon pines hang over the edge and one, a big one, had been hit by lightening and burned not too long ago. The powdery white ash has yet to blow away.

Then following courses water has made, we were careful not to walk on cryptobiotic soil, where weird black algal and fungal combinations grow like huge crystals. Then we moved through five acres of yellow grasses (*Oryzopsis* or *Hilaria*) that brushed our shins like soft hair, and big, shoulder-high sage and perfect ephedra and deer tracks by the millions and a few of their bones with coyote scat next to them. And then we saw the grandpa juniper with dry berries piled high at its base.

Bob and I talk while we sort through handfuls of duff on one side of the huge tree. We talk about ghost beads, about keeping only the ones with holes. I wish I'd had some ghost beads last night. Then we talk about grazing and how I'm not against it, not really, but raising cows here in the desert doesn't seem right. Two days ago I heard Marc Reisner, author of *Cadillac Desert*, talk about cows and water. He said that one pound of beef requires thousands of gallons of water and that only three per cent of the nation's beef is raised on western public lands—meaning no one would notice if all our cows were shipped to Florida to eat non-irrigated knee-high grass.

Besides twigs, soil, two small bones, round rat scat, flat pieces of rock, and dry ephedra, I count 87 ghost beads in one handful of duff. We quickly gather enough seeds for two necklaces and then we get up and start walking.

We walk for another long dreamy hour in paths shaped like question marks to avoid leaving evidence of our presence. A troubling feeling surfaces inside me. At first it is like a curious fear, like a child's mixed with the excitement of a new, mysterious place he has found but doesn't belong. Then I feel that this mesa has stopped doing what it has been doing uninterrupted for a hundred-thousand years to watch us. I'm thinking to myself that we don't belong here and although I can't see the murkiness I've caused, I feel as if I've walked through a clear pond and only with time will it settle out.

If a place can have a soul, and I believe that it can, this place does, a secret soul that cows would love to eat and trample, and even being careful, our presence here is wrong. This is not a national park, not designated wilderness. But it is special simply because it is as it has always been.

We are worried about leaving too many footprints so we angle away from the center of the mesa to its western edge. This side drops further, cut by the front edge of a million years of weather. Below us, huge Kayenta Sandstone fins stretch out like red braces holding this mesa in place. We find our way down the Navajo Sandstone and onto one Kayenta fin. It is dangerous, but I feel better about not going back across the mesa and interrupting it again. When it gets steep we use our rope to help us down. We move quickly in and out of the canyon tops formed by water pouring off the mesa, leading to the Colorado River and then to Mexico. The country flattens out again and there are more

cow pies than grass and rain has cut deep arroyos and we wonder about the arrogance of people who have taken only one hundred years to change the entire history of this place. We cut around the south end of the mesa and there is the road and then the car. I wonder again about my dream and letting go.

I realize, driving away, that I've learned something about history; that it is not then and now. We are not separate from history. Our footprints up there on that mesa are now part of its history. History, especially natural history, is constant, like a current. Maybe we should quit differentiating between "history" and "natural history." The future will have questions for us. Leaving this mesa alone will look good to the future. It is good to wonder about, and good to know that there are places in Utah with no cows, where just two sets of human footprints can disturb the peace. It is good to know there are places with beads that can help us with our dreams.

CLARET CUP CACTUS IN COURTHOUSE WASH, ARCHES NATIONAL PARK

PINNACLE IN INDIAN CREEK DRAINAGE, PROPOSED CANYONLANDS BASIN WILDERNESS

94

Bristlecone pine trees are among the earth's oldest living things. Though probably long dead, this gnarled specimen still lifts its arms to the sky in the Ashdown Gorge Wilderness of Dixie National Forest. Growing on exposed, cold, and windy ridges, these unique and beautiful pines seem to thrive on adversity. Forests of the bristlecone pines occur at high elevation on several of the Great Basin ranges of western Utah, including Notch Peak near Delta and throughout the Deep Creek Mountains south and east of the Great Salt Lake Desert.

**BRISTLECONE PINE,
ASHDOWN GORGE WILDERNESS**

REED PATTERN IN NEGRO BILL CANYON, PROPOSED LA SAL WATERS WILDERNESS

OPPOSITE: PLUNGE POOL REFLECTION, GLEN CANYON NATIONAL RECREATION AREA

LILY PADS IN BUTTERFLY LAKE, WASATCH-CACHE NATIONAL FOREST

PREVIOUS PAGE: FERN-COVERED ALCOVE ALONG SAM'S MESA BOX CANYON, PROPOSED DIRTY DEVIL WILDERNESS

MONKEYFLOWERS IN BLOOM, HIGH UINTAS WILDERNESS

Spring touches the lower slopes of Mount
Nebo while winter lingers on the higher
ramparts of the Mount Nebo Wilderness.
A landmark that can be seen for great
distances in all directions, Mount Nebo
stands nearly 12,000 feet, the highest
peak of the Wasatch Range. The Mount
Nebo of the holy land in Jordan is a
rather unimposing desert hill, but there
are similarities. While Mount Nebo in
Utah provides fine views of Utah Lake
and the Great Salt Lake, its counterpoint
in the Middle East affords vistas of the
Dead Sea, and on clear days, it is possible
to see the biblical land of Moab.

**ASPEN GROVE BELOW MOUNT NEBO,
MOUNT NEBO WILDERNESS**

In Utah, time begins where the dark rocky heart of Westwater Canyon throbs in the heat. I am standing balanced on a curved, eroded edge tying our bowline around the only boulder with a chance of holding our boat while we eat lunch. One slip and big wild water will sweep me away, the same water that has carved these walls for a billion years into what seem to be the smooth and visceral innards of a huge animal.

I feel swallowed.

"We" are Tom Till, photographer and boatman, and our guide Karla VanderZanden, a former Westwater river ranger and current executive director of the Canyonlands Field Institute, and myself. I have come to see the beginning of Utah history.

We have seen places where the schist is squared off and cut straight and looks like crystals under a microscope. In others, the river has worn organic, sensuous flutes, smooth and shiny and constantly wet. If I could break off a chunk and take it with me to suck on, I am sure I would never need water again.

But here the curved walls seem to be cut from one huge black rock, carved and holding the river like the bottom of a dark perfect tube. The weaving together of reflected and direct light attacks my eyes and my cheeks ache from squinting. Fifty feet up, living things like cottonwood trees and desert holly have found soil in the cracks. At my feet, a cone is carved in the rock with four pebbles in the bottom. It has a low point where the edge of the river enters, filling it up and spinning the stones in perfect circles, scratching against the sides. In all this hugeness I am witnessing the process of water sculpting this place, the important but undetectable work of one day.

It all began 1.8 billion years ago with shales that formed when layers of organic material were deposited on top of each other. Under heat and pressure from the weight of thousands of feet of sediments, and over all that time, these shales turned black and hard and became the core of this canyon.

In a sub-region of the Colorado Plateau, geologic forces slowly pushed the sediments to heights of 20,000 feet, creating the Uncompahgre Uplift. One-hundred-million years of erosion leveled it, leaving a gap in the geological record. Today, these black granite schists support the Chinle Formation, deposited 245 million years ago. It was about that same time that dinosaurs roamed the area. The seas and lakes and flood plains of the wet periods of this epoch became the Chinle, Carmel, and Morrison formations. The alternating dry, desert periods produced the Windgate, Navajo, and Entrada sandstones.

Beginning forty million years ago, the La Sal, Henry, and Abajo mountains were formed when volcanic activity pushed up semi-molten rocks. Then, the Uncompahgre Uplift was rising again, and, simultaneously, some of the sediments deposited by the flooding and receding of an enormous western sea were eroding away.

Fifteen million years ago, the entire Colorado Plateau was rising. As long as twelve million years ago—or as recently as two—the Westwater began as a small tributary of the ancestral Colorado River, whose main stem flowed through Unaweep Canyon, across the Uncompahgre Uplift. This tribu-

POLISHED ROCKS, SAN JUAN RIVER

OPPOSITE: WATER-SCULPTED SCHIST, WESTWATER CANYON, WESTWATER CANYON WILDERNESS STUDY AREA

HUGE WAVES BUFFET A RAFT IN CATARACT CANYON, CANYONLANDS NATIONAL PARK

OPPOSITE: THE COLORADO RIVER, FROM THE RIM OF WESTWATER CANYON,
WESTWATER CANYON WILDERNESS STUDY AREA

tary eroded headward through soft Mancos Shale, eventually capturing the entire river system. The area continued uplifting and the new river kept cutting deep, eventually exposing these dark rocks. I have read about these rocks for years, and I knew that any book about Utah's history would be incomplete without reference to the state's geologic beginnings.

A month ago, Tom and I made arrangements with Karla to run Westwater Canyon. The canyon is seventeen miles long, and most trips are done in one day. But we wanted to camp. By the time we pushed off, the sun's very last rays were bouncing around high on the cliffs. We floated an hour from the put-in point, past fifty great blue herons fishing at the edges, a hundred turkey vultures in a tree waiting for death, any death, a peregrine falcon, three sandpipers, and a kingfisher watching evening change the water.

We pulled over where a geologic fault had cut through the canyon, leaving a high beach. The huge Windgate wall had broken up into boulders that we climbed for a thousand feet to the top, where Tom waited for a photograph to emerge from a massive wall with the distant La Sal Mountains floating above it. We came down in the dark empty-handed when the light Tom hoped for didn't materialize.

At dawn we tried again. By the time we climbed the thousand feet and waited an hour for the right light, took the photo, and came back, the morning was mostly gone.

Wild Horse Rapid was first, just after the dark rock rose up around us on both sides. I had watched from the bow, beyond the silky tongue where the water is deepest but also the fastest, across the drop where the river disappears and all I could see was the crazy dance of the rapid's foam tails. I could smell the rapid and imagine fossil forests and the world's very first sand.

Brown Colorado River water somehow turns pink as it picks up speed when the canyon narrows, folding and bending and covering all the rock's hard edges, intimate and wet like hidden flesh. We had already run Big Hummer and Staircase, Marble Canyon (where a coyote swam the river between Karla's boat and ours, climbed out of the water, shook its stringy body and disappeared through a crack in the schist) and Little Dolores—all separated by short sections of simple silent water licking the dark rock.

These are all intense rapids—we can never hesitate. In Funnel Falls, water floods from three directions into a hole. Karla disappeared into the hole, only to pop up in an unpredictable place like driftwood. Tom and I weren't worried. Karla has been through this canyon four hundred times.

We stop here, between Funnel Falls and Surprise Rapids, to eat lunch and let Karla, who is paddling an inflatable kayak, take off her dry suit to let her body feel some new air.

Here, the deepest, dark and shiny past meets the present. In a way we've completed a circle and we want to sit here for a while, but we can't. There are more rapids to run, Skull and Sock-It-To-Me and then Last Chance will spit us out of the dark rock and the world will open back up and herons will be fishing there. I will row the last seven miles in water that could be a lake. It will be hard and I won't know exactly why—because my body is weak or old or tired or because we have been to the middle of gravity, the earth's magnet, and are feeling the firm and smooth pull of old, old rocks.

HONEYCOMB PATTERNS, DIRTY DEVIL RIVER

ABSTRACT DETAIL OF KANAB WONDERSTONE, KANAB

In the Nature Conservancy's Scott Matheson Wetlands Preserve near Moab, an old beaver lodge is left high and dry by receding river waters. This preserve is the only high-quality wetlands along the Colorado River in Utah. Encompassing nearly a thousand acres, it is home to over 150 species of birds, including eagles, ibis, egrets, and hawks. The preserve was dedicated in 1991 and is one of many projects by the Conservancy to protect and preserve the natural integrity of the state.

ABANDONED BEAVER LODGE, SCOTT MATHESON WETLANDS PRESERVE, NEAR MOAB

CACTUS AND PENSTEMON BLOOMS, PROPOSED ESCALANTE WILDERNESS

DESERT VARNISH ON A WALL ALONG THE ESCALANTE RIVER, PROPOSED ESCALANTE WILDERNESS

Seen from a canyon rim, the Colorado

River snakes toward Moab past Fisher

Towers and Castle Rock in the Richardson

Amphitheater. River runners delight

in this stretch of river, which includes

White's Rapid with its thundering hole,

and New Rapid, formed by flash floods

in 1976. Scenic Utah Highway 128, one

of America's most beautiful drives, follows

the river as it drops from Westwater Canyon

to Moab. Poetic names abound in this area:

the Priest and Nuns, the Titan, Polar Mesa,

and Ida Gulch are but a few.

**COLORADO RIVER AS IT FLOWS THROUGH
RICHARDSON AMPHITHEATER**

DINOSAUR TRACKS PRESERVED IN MOENAVE FORMATION, HURRICANE CLIFFS

GEYSER AND TRAVERTINE LEDGES, GREEN RIVER GEYSER

At Red Canyon Overlook, wet autumn

snow clings to the forest and canyon walls

above Flaming Gorge. The Green River

has been a focal point of Utah history

since ancient peoples carved huge petroglyphs

at Rainbow Park, near Split Mountain.

Flaming Gorge, Split Mountain, and

Rainbow Park are a few of the poetic

names bequeathed to the Green River by

John Wesley Powell, the greatest explorer

of Utah's eastern mountains and canyons.

**RED CANYON IN WINTER, FLAMING GORGE
NATIONAL RECREATION AREA**

THE FUTURE OF EXPERIENCE

A young, handsome couple comes towards me on the left edge of the pavement. She is in front, blonde. He is behind her with a baby in a teal blue carrier on his back and they smile when they pass. I walk around an older Asian couple who are stopping to look and point, and then two thin young men speaking German to each other. If I didn't know better I would think that this was an international pilgrimage and not the West Rim Trail in Zion National Park. But then, it might be both.

A half hour ago, after waiting fifteen minutes to find a parking place at the Grotto Picnic Area, six of us loaded our packs, with gear for three days, threw them up on our backs, and walked across the Virgin River bridge.

It is October, autumn in the desert, and our first mile is slow because of the parade. I am anxious to get beyond the crowds where I can lengthen my stride and pick up my pace.

This trail winds through broken Navajo Sandstone boulders, yucca, blackbrush, and oak, and then cuts into the huge wall forming the western side of this spectacular canyon, which attracts a million visitors every year. I follow it up switching back and forth, trying to breathe in rhythm with my steps as the trail gets steeper, toward the gap where it disappears into Refrigerator Canyon. It is so steep that grooves have been added for traction. A deer tried the trail before the cement was dry.

The trail eases and I enter the canyon, which feels humid and junglelike compared to the dry desert, and wet smells flood past me mingled with breezes.

Earlier, while waiting for my friends in Springdale, I saw the film "The Treasure of the Gods" in the new IMAX Theater, just south of the park entrance. The theater was a source of controversy for years before it was built. I was against it, wondering why visitors needed anything more than the real park wonders and what a six-story building would do to the profile of the area. Well, my worst fears were not completely realized. They sunk a few of the stories into the ground and the building is no taller than the orange and purple butte next to it. It is painted rusty red to fit in, but it is still huge. Besides watching the film, visitors can buy food, books, and souvenirs there, have their film developed in one hour, and get cash from a Zions Bank ATM.

I sat down exactly in the middle of the squeaky clean theater, which smelled like a new car. Four other people came in and the film began with a stewardess voice explaining the technology. The images coming from film are ten times the normal size—the world's largest motion picture screen. The voice also made the disclaimer that while most of the film was made in Zion, there were also scenes from Bryce, Canyonlands, Mesa Verde, and other parks.

The film is high tech and beautiful. It is a fictional story of gold lost, found, lost, and found again. There is a ceremonial scene from inside an Anasazi kiva, similar to the one my modern white mind made up in the perfect kiva that Glen and I found. There are slot canyons like some I've been in, incredible footage shot from the air, and a flash flood that sweeps a nineteenth-century photographer away.

MOON ABOVE DELICATE ARCH,
ARCHES NATIONAL PARK

Grandview Point forms the southern
end of Island in the Sky in Canyonlands
National Park. A view of epic proportions
even by Utah standards, the name refers
to more than just scenic grandeur. Until
early this century, the Colorado River
was called the Grand River, becoming the
Colorado only below its confluence with
the Green River, thousands of feet beneath
Grandview Point. Many names in eastern
Utah and western Colorado, including
Grand County and Grand Junction, still
reflect the original name.

RAINBOW OVER CANYONLANDS NATIONAL PARK

AUTUMN COLOR, ZION NATIONAL PARK

As I walked out of the dark theater, past the three busloads of elderly tourists on their way in, I couldn't help but wonder if after they've seen the film, they might think it is a good substitute for the real thing. Part of me wanted to scream when the sun hit me in the face.

I hike the Refrigerator Canyon part of the trail figuring that in the time we will be gone the film will be shown forty-eight times.

Hiking is a good way to think. The rhythm of movement combines with all the wonders surrounding me to poke deep into the middle of my brain. My mind wanders and things that might seem unrelated at first begin to line up and make a long row of sense. But tomorrow, away from the trails, in that wild deep secret place, there won't be much thinking. A trail means transportation and isolation. Off trail means integration and attention, which is more than thinking. Much more.

I climb Walter's Wiggles eternal switchbacks quickly, knowing I can rest at the top. This engineering wonder was built during the Depression by the Civilian Conservation Corps, as were many of Zion's trails. I stand on a familiar boulder on the edge of the canyon, just beyond where the trail splits at the top. We will go left, up higher on the rim. Going right takes hikers up to Angels Landing on a thin path pecked into the rock, so exposed that chains and handrails have been added. A thousand feet down I can see the Virgin River and the road and, across the canyon, the side of the Great White Throne. I came here often as a park ranger in the mid-seventies. I love the massy sandstone.

Usually when I think of Zion, this rock is where my mind takes me: Navajo Sandstone in every color of orange and sometimes white. How solid I feel when I stand there and look out on a world where I feel alive, the wonder and the wet air on my face, the swift breeze cooling my sweaty back and blowing air through the bottom of my lungs.

This is different than the film.

But this last year my thoughts of Zion are of news footage taken from the air above Kolob Creek, a white gash in a green landscape where three men and five Venture Scouts from a Mormon ward in Salt Lake City went hiking last year. Two of the men died and the rest were stranded five days waiting for rescue when the water in the creek rose unexpectedly. And now the survivors are suing the government for $26 million because Park Service employees didn't stop them from going, didn't protect them from themselves. By the time this is published, the case might be resolved. If the survivors win, we will all be pretending the government is responsible for us in the wilds and we'll be sneaking into off-limits, unknown places. If the government wins, we'll still be on our own.

MAPLE PALETTE, MILL CREEK CANYON,
WASATCH NATIONAL FOREST

Here in Zion, in the brilliant fall, I think about the future. Not just Zion, but the orange hoodoos of Bryce and the silty castles and open spaces of Capital Reef, the rock-planet Canyonlands and the miracles in Arches and all the monuments and wilderness areas that as Americans, we all own. Will these places be reduced to museums dedicated to what we've lost, ignored, or given away? Places to watch perfect movies filmed on perfect days, or to pay homage by walking only on paved trails with safety rails using bodies that have become faint shadows of themselves?

No. I believe we are waking up. We are beginning to consider not only the full extent of what is known, but also what is unknown. We can see that we are a bigger people when we know our deepest history, the one that goes back beyond people whose names we know, down and down through the dirt and red rocks to our own wet black core, where experience transcends meaning. We need to do the work that will assure us that our public lands will always have room for hidden, left-alone places to house our spirits, where secrets are stored and all the elements intact. History is not something to learn as much as it is something to live.

My friends catch up and we rest and drink and then climb the trail to the top, another hour or two. Then we camp in the shadows and cook and sleep while our water freezes. In the

morning we sneak through the ponderosa pine forest (smell them!) to a wide, white sandstone ramp. We slip off the side, through white and brown dirt and blood-barked manzanita. We wrap our rope around a tree and slide down it to a different, new world. Actually it is a very old world, one where we can survive, even thrive, using faint echoes of the same skills our species used for over a million years to get us here. We climb down tilted rock and follow deer between trees too big to hug our arms around, to dry washes where the only marks are lion prints and the perfect circles of grasses spun by the wind.

INTENSE PINKS OF A STORMY DAWN, BRYCE CANYON NATIONAL PARK

OPPOSITE: SUNRISE WARMS A SNOWY MORNING, BRYCE CANYON NATIONAL PARK

BALANCED ROCK PANORAMA, ARCHES NATIONAL PARK

LIGHTNING ABOVE BALANCED ROCK, ARCHES NATIONAL PARK

ENTRADA SANDSTONE OF NORTH WINDOW FRAMES A FULL MOON, ARCHES NATIONAL PARK

PRINCES PLUME ON GREEN RIVER OVERLOOK, CANYONLANDS NATIONAL PARK

MESA ARCH, CANYONLANDS NATIONAL PARK

136

Another magnificent dawn graces

Monument Valley Tribal Park along

the Utah/Arizona border. More open

than much of the surrounding canyon

country, Monument Valley is famous for

its sunrises and sunsets, usually draw-

ing large crowds at overlooks for both.

Like much of southern Utah, the area

is also a magnet for large numbers of

foreign tourists and the advertising

industry, which has used the Mittens,

one of which is pictured here, in

countless advertisements for countless

products. Photographers, of course, find

the landscape irresistible, a combina-

tion of the world's best lighting and the

earth's grandest gestures.

**NORTH MITTEN,
MONUMENT VALLEY TRIBAL PARK**

DESERT PAINTBRUSH AND CLIFFROSE, ARCHES NATIONAL PARK

OPPOSITE: PAUL BUNYAN'S WOODPILE, COLUMNAR BASALT FORMATIONS
ON BLM WEST DESERT LANDS

FALLS ALONG THE FREMONT RIVER, CAPITOL REEF NATIONAL PARK

LAKE POWELL AT DAWN, GLEN CANYON NATIONAL RECREATION AREA

At Muley Point in Glen Canyon National Recreational Area, the San Juan River meanders through narrow canyons toward Lake Powell. On this, the southern rim of Cedar Mesa, millions of years of geology are revealed. Downstream a few miles, hikers can see geology in the making. A huge new waterfall on the river has been born, caused by the river seeking to bypass the silt left by Lake Powell. Though the huge cascade will be very shortlived in geologic time, the river seems to be temporarily reasserting itself, seeking any way it can to find its old way to the ocean.

**MULEY POINT, GLEN CANYON
NATIONAL RECREATION AREA**

A SPIRIT
REFRESHED

It's the world's most beautiful place. Though it's not politically correct to say it these days because of the hordes who may be drawn here by such talk, it's true. When I first came to Utah twenty years ago and immersed myself in the light and loneliness of the Colorado Plateau, I looked for a way to express my deep feelings for the captivating desert landscape. The humble craft of photography became my medium, launching me on an odyssey that will continue, I hope, until my life ends.

A critic once suggested that photographers are pushed away from nature by the act of photographing, that their attention to the technology and the capsulizing of nature onto a captured image detracted mightily from the enjoyment and true appreciation of nature. In my case, I honestly believe that photographing the natural world has blessed my life in countless ways. Besides the wonderful curiosity that photography engenders—a desire to know more about the history, geology, or botany of a photographed subject—a good photographic session can sometimes take on almost spiritual overtones.

During such periods time seems to speed up, with hours passing in mere moments. The mind and heart's attention is totally outward, attuned to the movements of clouds, the fortuitous assemblages of light and darkness, the smells of a fresh snowfall or of an atmosphere drunken with sagebrush. Pure instinct, born of countless similar experiences with stone, light, and cloud comes into play, directing the photographic response, while the spirit is refreshed by the heartbreaking beauty of the land.

Most often such experiences reach their peak for me during storms, and any perusal of my work will reveal a penchant for tempestuous conditions. A colleague once suggested jokingly that I could control the weather, but the opposite is really the truth. I chase storms, thunderstorm cells, and winter blizzards, trying to combine atmospheric pyrotechnics with a subject on the ground.

The challenges of working under such rapidly changing and difficult conditions help keep photographing nature a fresh and exciting job for me. When summer thunderstorms build up in the afternoon, I begin to plan an evening's work with anticipation and expectation. On a recent August evening I started a typical session by following an ebony cloud that developed over Arches National Park near my home in Moab. The blackest clouds offer some of the best opportunities for flash floods, storm light, and rainbows. Before I had even reached Arches, a rainbow appeared over the Colorado River Bridge, offering a stunning scene of the flame red waters underneath the arching bow. Unfortunately, the best view of the scene required walking out on the busy bridge, and by the time I had done so the momentary phenomenon was gone.

Flickering lightning over Spanish Valley indicated the storm was headed toward the southern end of the La Sal Mountains. Since I prefer to have an interesting subject to combine with the opportunities a storm can bring, I began thinking of natural features in the area of the storm's path. Wilson Arch, a beautiful span that could be reached quickly on the paved road (the storm's torrential rains had made leaving the pavement in any vehicle, or even on foot, almost impossible) came quickly to mind. I arrived at the arch as windblown rain continued to pelt my windshield. On the western horizon, though, a faint hope appeared. A tiny hole in the massive flotillas of clouds appeared where the sun might eventually shine through, so I settled down to patiently wait. Most times in situations like this, nothing happens, and I return home with no photographs. On this evening, however, I was lucky, as the sun and the small gash in the thunderheads aligned perfectly. The pelting rain and wind did not diminish as a rainbow appeared faultlessly splayed above the natural stone opening. As quickly as I wiped rainwater off the lens, the continuing downpour drowned out any chance of a photograph. Finally I rigged a small umbrella to cover the camera and quickly made an exposure before the rainbow faded forever.

A few days later, I assessed the results. My one chance had miraculously worked. The rainbow was situated exactly over the arch, and the photo was marred only by a small soft area were a raindrop had lodged during the exposure. A bit of luck, a smidgen of instinct, and a little craftsmanship had come together at the right moment. The picture has come to be one of my favorites, for I like the idea of the two natural arches, both miracles of nature, merging for a tiny moment, almost like the conjunction of two mighty planets.

The photograph has never been sold or published. Many of what I consider my best never are. They languish in my files, or go in and out of the office dozens of times without any attention from editors or the public. Since I'm left with the experience and an image that pleases me I don't really care. I'm very lucky. I spend my life exploring the hinterlands of Utah and other beautiful places seeking out the splendorous moments that come and go with the daily and yearly cycles of nature. I strive to be what author W. L. Rusho called the Utah mystic Everett Ruess—"a vagabond for beauty in the world's most beautiful place."

TOM TILL